CBT WORKl

7 Strategies To Manage And Overcome Anxiety, Depression, Anger, Panic, Worry, Intrusive Thoughts

Learn How To Regulate Emotions And Motivate Change

Mind Change Academy

Disclaimer Notice:

Please be aware that the information cont ned in this document is for educational and entertainment purpc ɛs only. All effort has been made to ensure accuracy, releva :e, and reliability. No guarantees are made or implied. Readɛ ; understand that the author is not providing legal, financial, 1edical or professional advice. The information in this book ha been gathered from a variety of sources. It is strongly encourage to seek the advice of a qualified professional before trying any tɛ 1niques outlined in this document.

By reading this document, the reader agi ɛs that the author shall not be held responsible for any losses, w ɛther direct or indirect, which may arise from the utilization of tɦ information within this document, including — but not limited to · mistakes, omissions, or misstatements.

Table of Contents

** BONUS 1 **

As a way of expressing my gratitude for your purchase, I am offering you a complimentary report that is only available to readers of this book

With EMOTIONAL DIARY you'll discover a printable reference journal of rules to know how to manage your emotions.

Writing all the emotions you feel is the first step to see their effect on your life, to understand them and finally manage them to live a more peaceful life.

Everything you need to get started with EMOTIONAL DIARY is to download your free diary.

Click this link to free download

https://dl.bookfunnel.com/x1qtousl6

Meditation Music

We have created a YouTube channel to give you the opportunity to listen to relaxing music to meditate, relax, study, work and sleep better.
The numerous beneficial effects of music on the human being have been confirmed by many scientific researches around the world. Listening to it increases the production of serotonin (a natural antidepressant), reduces the secretion of stress hormones (cortisol) and stimulates the production of beta-endorphins (analgesics produced by the body), acting as a real antidote against states of anxiety, insomnia and psychophysical fatigue.

Meditation music, for example, is a very effective tool for combating stress, easing tensions, alleviating the rhythms of modern life and bringing general well-being.

It also has a positive effect on feelings of depression, anxiety or loneliness, but a close relationship between music, cognitive processes and human mood has also been demonstrated.

These are just some of the benefits you can gain from listening to relaxing music for meditation:

- Relief from stress and anxiety
- Improves the quality of rest and sleep by calming the nerves and diverting attention from a noisy brain.
- Increases concentration and memory capacity
- Improves physical health by helping your body heal and rest
- Rebalances heart and respiratory function
- Reduces blood pressure levels
- Improves blood oxygenation through deep breathing

7

- Activates energy and vitality lev s
- Helps with positive thinking
- Increases self-awareness
- Stimulates creativity
- Instils self-esteem

YOUTUBE https://bit.ly dyv5u7

FACEBOOK **_https://bit.l_** **_3SWKlRB_**

Cognitive

Behavioral

Therapy

Introduction

What Is Cognitive Behavioral Therapy?

We have to face quite a few specific kinds of problems and events of life. Any of those might be nice; others might not be so fun. However, the way we live life, whether we love it or hate it, is a characteristic of the kind of perspective we have, as well as the emotional strength we can muster. Some individuals are always optimistic and positive, allowing them with power and equanimity to deal with all circumstances. There are others on the other end of the scale that are very timid and also negatively predisposed, making them quite scared, scared, and even quite intimidated by everything.

While in some other cases, some people are cynical by nature, people also go through traumatic experiences that change their lives forever. For example, children who experience a murder or possible terrorist attack could suffer lifelong mental damage and suffer from panic and anxiety attacks. To the point where they are eternally miserable or perhaps cranky, moody, and angry all the time, surely others feel harassed and bothered as well. These are all examples of behaviorally dysfunctional actions and lifestyles that need to be addressed through cognitive behavioral therapy, also known as CBT.

CBT is a therapy through which professional clinicians and psychologists work alongside people to try to help them find the reason they are behaving in a particular way with themselves. Thoughts provide a ride into build emotions and behavior and make it essential to address ideas and also analyze them properly so that the root cause of the problem can be identified and resolved. The fundamental strategy is to replace depressive feelings with constructive and optimistic feelings before the individual has a second nature, which is positivity. Only in this way can one be healthy and happy again.

We do not take for granted that CBT is a straightforward technique. Of one, it needs a lot of meticulous and long-drawn psychoanalysis methods, as well as psychiatric therapy such that old memories and deteriorating or wounded emotions will be allowed to disappear into the past. This will help bring happiness to the forefront, and help a person make rational and healthy choices too. After all, ensuring that life is lived to the fullest without regrets is crucial.

How Does CBT Work?

Cognitive-behavioral therapy has a six-phase approach to helping people heal their mental conditions that they are dealing with. The goal is to recognize the cognitive distortions that they are experiencing, and identify ways that they can overcome these cognitive distortions by ultimately creating stronger coping methods, cognition, emotions, and behaviors. The goal is to develop people who are more adaptive and capable of being involved in the real world with less problematic experiences in their emotions and cognitions.

The entire cycle of CBT starts with recognizing what the problematic behaviors and experiences are, and using those to identify the challenging cycles that people are facing in their minds, which lead to these actions and experiences. After that, the individual learns CBT-based techniques that are meant to help them navigate those thoughts, feelings, and behaviors healthily and more effectively. Through that, they can begin changing their problematic cycles, which results in them experiencing newer, less troubling processes in their lives.

Basic CBT Framework

CBT relies on a basic framework that follows six phases. These six phases are meant to draw a map for how the individual is going to get from where they are now to where they want to be. This entire forward-focus of CBT is what leads to individuals having such a great benefit from CBT as it supports them with coping and healing going forward, rather than placing excessive emphasis on what has happened in the past.

Phase One: Assessment

The first phase in CBT is to assess what the problem is and get a full scope understanding of what this problem is leading to an individual's life. The idea is to create a map of sorts that shows where the problem is starting and what it is leading to every single time it takes place. Usually, in this phase, people see that their issues are leading to situations that are causing more of the same problem to keep occurring. This can lead to people feeling like they are "stuck" or like there is no way for them to escape the cycle that they are living in, and so they seek treatment.

Getting a full and clear understanding of what the problem is and what the situation entails is essential, as this is the entire foundation upon which the individual will be able to begin changing their experiences. You need to make sure that you have everything in place and clearly understood, so that you can identify the proper strategies that are going to support you in healing the ailments that have caused you to seek treatment in the first place.

Phase Two: Reconceptualization

The next part of the CBT framework is reconceptualization. Often, once people identify the cycles of their problems, they realize that in their minds, they feel as though things could not possibly go in any other way. The idea is that the way things are now is unchangeable, and people will always continue to have these experiences and feel this way, and there is nothing that can be done about it. Of course, this same set of beliefs leads to them feeling trapped in the first place because they are incapable of seeing that there are other possibilities for how things could go or what could be done to break the cycle.

During the reconceptualization phase, the entire purpose is to identify what can be changed about the individual's present belief system to make one that is much more supportive of their goals in life. This way, they can begin to see beyond their limited perspective and limiting beliefs and start to see into a new truth or a new way of thinking that supports them in breaking the cycle. In some cases, the belief shift is slight, whereas, in others, an entirely new way of perceiving and believing may be required to help the person ultimately move on from that way of behaving.

Phase Three: Skills Acquisition

Now, the individual has identified the new goals and new way of perceiving their reality. They need to move into acquiring skills that can help them reinforce these new beliefs in their life. Often, people do not believe in a different way of life, because they do not have the skills needed actually to make that way of life exist, so they think that they are incapable of getting there. When you begin to create the skills, you need to have the reality you want to have, believing that it is possible and getting there becomes a lot easier. Also, changing your mind becomes a lot easier because you no longer feel trapped within your cycles, and instead start having hope in what you may experience in the future.

Phase Four: Skills Consolidation and Application

Once you have figured out which skills will work best for you when it comes to treating your ailment, and you've practiced them, you need to start consolidating and applying them to your actual condition. This is the part of your process where you get the opportunity to bring these skills all together into one treatment, and use them to help you change your mind completely.

As you begin to consolidate your skills, you need to identify how you can reasonably apply them to your ability to overcome your ailment. This means that you need to go back to the map you drew in phase one and identify where these skills would be best used. Then prepare yourself for those circumstances by laying out how and when you will apply your new skills. Once you have created these expectations around yourself and your treatment, you can begin to implement your new skills in these areas and allow yourself to start experiencing the benefits of them.

Phase Five: Generalization and Maintenance

After you have begun routinely applying your new skills to your particular ailment, the next phase is to focus on generalization and maintenance. This is the part of CBT where you begin to learn how to take these new skills and strategies and turn them into actual routine practices that you are going to apply to your life as a habit. This is how you can begin to embrace your changes more automatically.

In addition to embracing your changes in a systematic way for your existing ailments, you also want to learn how to generalize these skills, so that you can use them for many areas of your life. Since CBT primarily focuses on stress management and stress response, these techniques can be used in many ways for people.

Learning how to generalize your skills, and apply them to multiple areas of your life, can help minimize your present ailment while also supporting yourself in experiencing a healthier life overall

Phase Six: Post-Treatment Assessment

As you continue to apply your CBT treatment to your ailment, you need to make sure that you take the time to perform a post-treatment assessment, to see if your new skills are helping you or not. Your post-treatment assessment will be done many times over until the point where you find that you have experienced significant enough relief for an extended period, which ultimately proves that you are no longer struggling.

It is essential to understand that even when your assessment says you are "all better," you still need to implement and reinforce your new skills. If you go back to your old way of living and experiencing, immediately after realizing it, you will find yourself experiencing tremendous struggles in your life, as you face difficulties in your way of coping once again. You must always continue to embrace your new way of being, so that you can continue to overcome the problematic ailment, while at the same time, you are preventing the development of any future complicated disorders due to poor coping methods.

Chapter 1: Strategies to Identify and Break Negative Thought Patterns

What Are Automatic Thoughts?

Automatic thoughts are an important part of the Cognitive Behavioral Therapy (CBT) model. They are ideas or thoughts that come to mind quickly and easily, without much effort. These thoughts tend to be short and relevant to the present moment. They appear instinctively as soon as the occurrence. They do not require much contemplation or rationalization, but they can often seem to be logical. Some of these thoughts are completely reasonable, while others are known as "dysfunctional automatic thoughts".

If you think another idea is more relevant to the issue at hand, concentrate on that instead. Or, if you feel that the primary thought is not as important as other matters, put it to one side and focus on other perspectives that had a more powerful effect on your feelings.

Assess the intensity of the emotions that each of the automatic thoughts evoked and determine which ones had the most significant influence.

These types of dysfunctional ideas may originate from cognitive distortions, also known as "thought traps", which are essentially mistakes in our thought process.

Recognizing the typical patterns of automatic thoughts can help to modify them. By identifying the cognitive distortions associated with certain categories, it is possible to change the thoughts within that group. Writing down some of your automatic thoughts may be a useful exercise, and then look for a solution. Here, we list some of the most widespread cognitive distortions.

What Are Intrusive Thoughts?

We can experience intrusive thoughts that are unpleasant, worrying, or upsetting. These thoughts can be persistent and difficult to ignore, and they can cause distress and anxiety. Examples of intrusive thoughts include fear of being responsible for something bad happening, fear of losing control, or fear of being judged by others. They can also include negative self-talk or thoughts of self-harm.

Unwanted and troubling ideas or impulses that are difficult to stop or control, often causing distress, are known as intrusive thoughts. They can disrupt activities and the flow of thoughts, as well as induce feelings of guilt, fear, shame, confusion, and anxiety. Such thoughts are commonly associated with anxiety disorders, OCD, and PTSD, but can also arise independently.

Other types of intrusive thoughts can include worries about the future, excessive concern about mistakes, or mundane tasks. It is possible to address these intrusive thoughts by using different strategies, such as cognitive-behavioral therapy, mindfulness, and relaxation techniques.

These topics are commonly tackle in the context of Obsessive-Compulsive Disorder (OCD). Worry intrusions are anxious thoughts about what may happen in the future or the potential for dange. Utilizing Cognitive Behavioral Therapy (CBT) methods may assist in decreasing the amount and intensy of these worries. Memories of a violent act or accident, a feeling of helplessness or fear during a traumatic experience, flashbacks of an intense moment, intrusive images of a traumatic event.

Trauma-induced recollections are unexpected recollections of past traumat occurrences or situations. Working collaboratively with a therapist to examine the sentiment affiliated with these memories can frequently aid in lessening their regularity.

Examples of Invasive Thoughts:

- Dealing with sexual thoughts involving a family member, child, or animal an be extremely challenging. (obsessional intrusn)
- Dealing with unwanted roman c advances from a coworker who does not reciproc te your feelings can be challenging. (obsessional int sion)
- Having thoughts of committin an abhorrent act, such as killing your spouse or arming your infant, can be quite distressing and al rming. (obsessional intrusion)

- Fear that you won't be able to stop yourself from saying something inappropriate in public. (obsessional intrusion)
- Anxiety that you have stopped subscribing to your faith, contemplated something forbidden for a short period of time, or done a duty incorrectly. (obsessional intrusion)
- Rehashed and strongly felt questions concerning your capacity to act on an up and coming test you have contemplated for. (worry intrusion)
- Rehashed and distressing musings about contracting a uncommon sickness and biting the dust. (worry intrusion)
- Rehashed contemplations about an embarrassing occasion that occurred in youth. (trauma-related intrusion)
- Unpleasant and disturbing memories of a traumatic event that happened during your adult years. (trauma-related)

These are just a few of the numerous ways intrusive thoughts can be expressed. Individuals are usually shocked to find out that there are other people who have experienced similar intrusive thought processes. Knowing this can be a source of comfort, helping you to understand that intrusive thoughts are a normal occurrence and not an indication of some kind of illness or error.

Most people have intrusive thoughts, but different people have varied reactions to them. The difference between those who struggle with intrusive thoughts and those who don't is not necessarily hat the latter don't have them, though it's possible t y experience them less often or with less intensity. R her, it's that those who don't have an issue with the oughts are able to ignore or reject them as not being meaningful or worth giving attention to.

People who struggle with obsessiv thoughts are likely to attach a lot of importance to t e ideas they have, and come to the conclusion that ey must believe or feel those things or will commit th se acts. They begin to create a narrative surrounding e ideas, which can involve questions about their chai cter, behavior, and what they will do in the future.

It's important to understand th t just because a thought or image pops into yo head, it doesn't necessarily mean it's true. Having such thoughts does not necessarily mean that you will t on them, or even that you want to. If you are spiritua y inclined, having a thought that goes against your be efs does not mean you actually believe it. If you are orrying excessively about a future event, the thoughts ou are having may not be based on reality and the ou ome you are afraid of may not be likely to happen.

Dr. Steven Phillipson is a renowne expert in this field. He often reminds his patients that hey do not have a "mental illness" but rather an a xiety disorder. He prefers to refer to intrusive th ights as "creative associations". This approach help patients to accept and feel comfortable with the frec ent and sometimes worrying thoughts. To find out more about Dr. Phillipson and his work, search "Dr. Phillipson OCD" on YouTube.

If intrusive thoughts are causing you anguish, make sure to include them as part of the explanation of the difficulty you are having.

Negative Thought Patterns

Cognitive-behavioral therapy is a research-backed approach to mental wellbeing which concentrates on our thoughts and how they influence our actions and emotions. CBT instructs us that we all have a variety of instinctive negative thought patterns that shape how we understand the world. When these negative thought patterns become dominant in our thinking, our stress can increase drastically.

There are several different types of automatic negative thought patterns associated with anxiety. The three that are the most problematic are:

- **Black-and-white thinking.** This type of thinking is referred to as "all-or-nothing" thinking. When we think in this way, there is no opportunity to consider other possibilities. For example, someone might believe that because they have been struggling with anxiety for a long period of time, that it is impossible for them to lessen it.

- **Over-generalizing**. This involves taking one problem and exaggerating it, making it bigger, so it applies to all areas of life. One mistake at work means that you are bad at everything.

23

- **_Jumping to conclusions_**. With this pessimistic outlook, you might be tempted to jump to conclusions about what someone else is thinking, believing that they would never accept an invitation to go on a date with you, or you might be inclined to make predictions about what negative outcome may occur in the future.

When you observe your thoughts without being critical of them, you could start to see some trends. Are you someone who likes to think in absolutes? Do you have a tendency to guess what other people are thinking? Pay attention to the subject matter of your thoughts as well as the type of thinking that is behind them. This will help you to recognize yourself and modify the way you are thinking.

The Solution: Seeing Our Thoughts Objectively

Why do our ideas seem to accumulate so quickly? Why does it happen that we can go from observing a stomachache to ringing our doctor, believing we have a bleeding ulcer in no time at all? This is partially due to the fact that we usually don't spend much time analyzing the characteristics of our thoughts or assessing how reasonable they are we just have them and then respond.

Gaining the ability to observe your own thoughts more objectively will enable you to gradually separate yourself from them, which can be very liberating! Acknowledging thoughts for what they are - transient ideas and impressions that will soon be replaced with the following thought that pops into your head – can help break the habit of mistaking thoughts for reality.

To facilitate this process, let's examine some of the most common misapprehensions concerning thoughts.

Unlike emotions, thoughts are factual. FALSE!

It's easy to forget that thoughts aren't facts. People often take their thoughts as absolute truths without question. But more often than not, our thoughts are neither accurate nor impartial. For example, take this scenario: you're walking down the hallway in your place of work, saying hello to your boss as you pass, but she doesn't even acknowledge you.

Your anxious thoughts make you feel like you have done something wrong and made her mad, even that you could get fired. You spend the whole day feeling very anxious. What your thoughts don't realize is that her boss had asked your boss to come, and she was on her way to a vital meeting. Distracted, she didn't hear your greeting. Your thoughts may have seemed real to you, but they were actually wrong.

Our thoughts about events around us accurately reflect the events themselves. FALSE!

Our interpretations of what is occurring in our environment are not the same as the reality of the situation. Our thoughts are merely our subjective understanding of the situation, not a factual representation of what is happening. Unfortunately, it is common for us to give our interpretations of the events the same importance as the actual events, which can lead to feelings of anxiety.

For instance, you witness your companion hugging someone else. Your mind is full of anxious thoughts, making you think that your partner might be unfaithful. In reality, the person you love is offering comfort to a colleague whose pet passed away the day before. The experience and your apprehensive ideas related to the event are two distinct things.

Our thoughts fill in the gap between what people say and what people mean. FALSE!

Our minds attempt to fill in the blanks, however frequently, there are no blanks to fill. Or if there are, our thoughts can't understand what's intended to be in the spaces.

Watching Your Thoughts Float Away

We tend to focus all our attention on our worries and anxieties when we struggle with them. Instead of engaging with these thoughts, debating with them, or trusting them, try to step away from them.

Create some space between yourself and your anxious thoughts by allowing them to pass without giving them your attention. Although it's inevitable that anxious thoughts will come up, don't let them take control of your focus; instead, just let them drift away.

Exercise

LET YOUR THOUGHTS FLOAT AWAY (12 MINUTES)

Practice this mindfulness meditation to learn how to observe your thoughts and let them drift away easily.

1. Find a comfortable place to sit or lie down.
2. Set a timer for 12 minutes.
3. Close your eyes and take some slow, deep breaths, inhaling and exhaling.
4. Imagine yourself on a sunny day, sitting in a grassy field, surrounded by dandelion tufts that have gone to seed and become round, white and fluffy.
5. Imagine yourself picking a dandelion and holding it in front of your face.
6. When a thought arises, imagine that thought floating away from you on a dandelion.
7. Take a deep breath in and then exhale strongly, dispersing your worries and thoughts into the wind like white dandelion seeds. (Note: Even though you may be imagining the image of the dandelion, take the time to really breathe in and out as if you were actually blowing away the seeds.)
8. Watch your thoughts drift away into the sky, don't attempt to chase them or make them leave your mind. Just observe them as they fly away.

9. Choose a new flower and repeat the steps until the time is up. Carry on if you want.

10. Your mind might be producing ideas faster than you can dismiss them, especially when you first start. That's alright. Keep breathing, blowing out, and observing your thoughts drift away.

11. Anxiety often stops us from having a good time, so let's add a fun element to the activity. Instead of imagining a dandelion puff, let's physically blow bubbles and watch as our thoughts drift away and burst.

The key to managing anxiety and overthinking is to direct your attention to the present moment. Rather than fighting against your anxious thoughts, accept the moment you're in. Surprisingly, with mindfulness, you won't need to block your thoughts or debate with them. Even though it might seem like trying to resist anxiety is the best solution, it never actually works.

If you've ever attempted to stop a child from having a meltdown by telling them to "stop it" or by offering counterarguments, you'll know that trying to fight the issue only exacerbates the behavior you want to put an end to. This can be likened to the anxious thoughts that can sometimes plague our minds they can be similar to toddlers throwing tantrums. The more we try to fight them, the louder and more persistent they become.

Instead of training your mind to be focused on what happened in the past or what may happen in the future, practice being aware of what's happening right now. Even though anxious thoughts may still be there, you

28

will be paying less attention to them. Just like a toddler, these thoughts need attention, but when you don't give it to them, they will gradually become weaker. As you become better at being aware of yourself and your environment, this skill will help you find balance and reduce anxiety. Anxiety is usually focused on what happened in the past or the future, but awareness is focused on the present.

To cultivate present moment awareness, purposefully focus your attention on the present moment with as many senses as you can. Our thoughts can often get in the way of our ability to experience life in all its sensory richness. However, if we make an effort to be mindful of our current environment, the sounds, sights and smells we experience can help to shift our anxious thoughts to ones that are more focused.

Awareness is a useful instrument to control your ideas, reduce nervousness and concentrate completely on what you are doing in the present. By doing this, you will cultivate a sense of serenity, balance and happiness - things that are much more pleasant and enjoyable than worrying about what happened in the past or what could occur in the future.

One final reminder before we begin studying the exercises: You will have the chance to learn and practice a variety of mindfulness activities as you go through this book. To maximize your experience, here are a few key suggestions.

- Include the ideas of not passing judgement, being patient and having an open mind.
- There is no definite answer that is either right or wrong when doing these exercises. Being mindful does not mean getting rid of all worries or thoughts that come to mind. It is the act of bringing our focus back to the current moment instead of getting caught up in anxiousness or continuous thinking.
- The goal is not to win against anxiety or to force any particular way of thinking. Instead, you should gradually incorporate a new way of living that, as a result, will reduce your anxiety.

Just exist — let things be the way they are, including yourself.

Chapter 2: Strategies for Managing and Overcoming Excessive Anger

We all get angry from time to time; it happens. When things don't go as planned or might not go as planned, you may find yourself becoming angry. However, this can get in the way of living your best life. If you find yourself constantly feeling angry, you may take time away from your happiness, and your life won't be as peaceful as a result. It's important to learn how to properly manage your emotions, so that you can make the most out of your day. Sometimes, we tend to overreact to certain situations. Although it's normal to feel these emotions, it can prove very helpful to learn how to handle them the best way. You may learn about why you get angry, as there are many reasons why this can happen. Learning about your anger can help you to become more aware of it. Then, you can learn how to stop feeling so angry all the time and instead learn how to handle it. You can react better to it and work on preventing yourself from becoming mad in the first place.

What Causes Anger?

Of course, everyone has different people, situations, and circumstances that make them angry. It comes and goes in waves, and sometimes it can get quite intense. If it gets particularly intense, you may lose control of yourself and the way you react. Anger can affect both you and those around you, and it may make it harder for you to properly deal with situations. You may justify your anger or feel the need to show it to get your way. Some even believe that it is a better way to show your feelings, as it is a "powerful" emotion. This emotion can have a very negative effect on you, and it's important to understand why it happens and what causes it.

Anger is an instinctual emotion. It is the way that one will respond to a perceived threat, and it can make you feel tense and increase your heart rate. When you're angry, your body will try to get you to fight whatever it is that's upsetting you or causing you to feel stressed. Although it can be helpful in some ways and at certain times, it certainly isn't the best way to respond to every situation that comes your way.

There are several triggers for anger. You may become angry as a result of impatience. Perhaps you are in a line, waiting for something to happen, or someone is late. You may become upset that things aren't going to plan and become angry as a result. Anger can also result from sadness. You may feel disappointed in someone or something. Perhaps somebody criticized you, and you took it personally. You may initially feel sad or generally upset with something that happened. Then, you may use anger as your way to deal with what's upsetting you. Instead of feeling sorry for being criticized, you can get mad at the person who said it for saying it in the first place. Anger can also result from memories of upsetting events such as trauma or even smaller events. Perhaps you think about that person that cut you off on the highway or about the time that your friend was late for your birthday celebration. It isn't even necessary for something to be happening at the exact moment that you're in for you to feel anger. It can result simply from a memory of something that previously upset you. Irritation can also occur as a result of the future. Perhaps you are upset that you aren't in control of your life or can't know what will happen.

Anger is also very individual. One may become angry over somebody chewing with their mouth open, while another may not care at all. You will have individual triggers that result from your personal preferences. Triggers may also be influenced by outside factors such as the way that you were raised, people that you surround yourself with, and your environment. You may learn how to handle your problem from those around you as well.

Stopping and Preventing Anger

It may seem like it is good for you to get your anger out every once in a while; however, it's even more important to be able to properly manage your anger. It isn't healthy for you to take your rage out on others. It also isn't healthy for you to get angry very often or for long periods of time. You must learn how to cool off when you're mad and how to stop yourself from becoming angry in the first place. Discovering how to handle your anger can really help you to live your best life and be happier.

There are a few ways that you can manage your anger. You may try to express your anger and let it out. This may involve you talking to somebody about what's upsetting you or writing down how you feel. It could also involve finding an outlet for you to let it out. You may consider doing some sort of physical activity such as boxing or running to use your emotions to your advantage. Expressing your anger can also have an unhealthy side. You may resort to having violent physical or verbal outbursts. Perhaps you take your anger out on others by putting them down or treating them poorly. Some deal with their anger by throwing or slamming things. It's important to be able to choose a healthy way to express your anger if you desire to say it when it occurs.

Another way that some choose to deal with their anger is through suppression. This is an unhealthy way to cope with your anger, as you aren't actually facing it and solving any problems. Instead of helping yourself to cope with it in a healthy way, you are choosing to ignore the emotion and attempting to hide it from yourself and others. This can result in an even worse feeling of anger later. It may also cause you to keep the anger in and turn it on yourself. When you do this, it will cause you to be angry at yourself and view yourself in a more negative light. You may also try to suppress it but be unsuccessful. Others can still notice it when you are sarcastic or passive-aggressive. It's better to recognize your emotions instead of trying to ignore them.

You may also try to calm down. ˥ is is different from suppressing your emotions. You re ɔgnize that you are angry and wish to help yourself to et in a better state of mind. It's important to find wha calms you down. It might be expressing your angɛ or sharing your emotions with others. There are ɪ any ways to relax, and it will be different for everyɔ ɪe. Some prefer to take a nice, warm bath to calm ɹown. Perhaps you enjoy meditating or simply being i silence so that you may focus and relax. There may bɛ ɪ hobby or mindless activity that you prefer to do. Musi can be a great way to calm yourself down.

Chapter 3: Strategies to Work through Worry, Anxiety, Fear, Panic, and Depression

Cognitive behavior follows a specific system that allows you to effectively implement this practice and experience full relief through your efforts. It starts by having you identify what the original thought processes are that are creating your unwanted emotional response, and then moves into you finding a way to interrupt those thoughts so that you can eliminate unwanted behaviors.

When you can identify the primary reason as to why you are experiencing emotional responses to your environment, you can easily begin to change it and allow yourself to grow beyond your anxiety, and depression.

As you work through the following five steps, realize that you will need to apply them to every single trigger that you experience, so that you can fully eliminate all of your emotional triggers.

This can take some time, particularly if you have been struggling for a significant amount of time, because there may be many triggers for you to work through. Furthermore, it will take several run-throughs of each stimulus to retrain your brain to respond in a new way versus the way that it has been reacting all along.

If you want to experience complete relief from your anxiety and depression, however, you will need to keep your faith and continue the process even when it doesn't seem like it's working, as it may take some time for your brain to adjust.

The more you run through your new reaction to your triggers, the more you will experience relief from your anxiety and depression. For that reason, you must go through the new motions even if it does not feel like they are working because, even though you cannot feel immediate results, they are.

Furthermore, to help you experience full relief, you should focus on working on your biggest triggers first and then moving on to manage smaller triggers later.

Attempting to override every trigger right off the bat can be overwhelming and may result in you struggling to maintain your changes. By focusing on your biggest things first, you can eliminate your overwhelming triggers and find yourself feeling significant relief rather quickly.

You might find that, through this, some of your smaller triggers naturally dissolve because you are no longer living in such a high state of overwhelm and stress.

Once these larger stresses are out of the way, if you find yourself dealing with any residual triggers, you can approach them in the very same way so that you can eliminate them as well. That way, you can experience complete relief from your anxiety or depression.

Step 1: Locate the Root Problem

The first step in coping with anxiety or depression through CBT is to identify the root problem that is responsible for causing your anxious or depressive episodes. In CBT, this root problem refers to the environmental condition that is causing you to have a specific about that condition, which subsequently leads to your emotional experiences.

The best way to begin identifying your root problem or problems is to sit down with a journal and write down everything that makes you feel either anxious or depressed. Be very clear on the specifics around these experiences so that you know exactly what it is that is stimulating your unwanted emotional response.

For example, if your family makes you anxious, be very clear on which family members are causing your anxiety and what it is that they are doing, which results in you experiencing your anxious responses. This clarity will ensure that you can pinpoint the exact moment that anxiety begins in your everyday experiences with these individuals.

That ability to pinpoint the exact moment will give you the awareness you need to identify the moment in action so that you can apply your other CBT practices to help you overcome your responses.

Make sure that you are exhaustive with this list, even if you are not planning on addressing every single circumstance right away. Developing awareness around what is causing you to generate these feelings is an important part of being able to effectively mitigate your response to the environmental experience itself.

Creating specific goals will ensure that you know exactly what actions you want to avoid repeating and what new behaviors you want to replace your old ones with. This will ensure that you can see just how far you are progressing and that you can make adjustments along the way if you find that you are not progressing as quickly as you would like to.

After you have created your goals, the next thing you need to do is to identify exactly what is going on in your mind when the root cause of your emotions is occurring. Ask yourself what thoughts you are having during those experiences and how those thoughts are contributing to the development of your anxiety.

For example, maybe when you experience anxiety from your boss wanting to talk to you, your immediate thoughts are, "What have I done wrong? Why can I never do anything right? I'm going to get fired, I won't be able to afford rent or food, I'm going to be homeless and hungry! Why can't I do anything right?"

These thoughts will trigger an anxious response because your immediate fear is that you are somehow going to be in danger of losing your living and the lifestyle that you have created for yourself. If you are unaware of the exact thoughts that you are experiencing, you might consider using a thought record, which is a tool that is commonly used in CBT.

The thought record allows you t record your ideas during your anxious experiences, s that you can begin to identify exactly what it is that yc are experiencing in your moments of anxiety. On your hought record, you need to include the time, the exter al trigger, the idea, the intensity of the thought, and e intensity of your emotional response.

Keeping a record of these can hel you identify where your troubling experiences lie an what you need to adjust in your mind through t e CBT process to eliminate your anxious responses. ou might consider using the thought record througho the entire process to help you track your improveme s if you are finding it difficult to see your own growth v hin yourself.

Step 2: Write Self-Stateme ts

Self-statements refer to the tho ghts that you are experiencing in your mind regardi yourself and how you view yourself in various circum ances in your life.

Our self-statements are general divided into two categories — positive and neg ive. Positive self-statements are how we reinforce (rselves from within and essentially praise ourselves fo ositive behavior or for something that we feel we did r ht.

For example, if you were praise by your boss for having done a great job on a rece project, your self-statements might be, "Wow, I am good at what I do! I'm a great person!".

Alternatively, negative self-statements are how we reprimand ourselves for doing something that we believe was done poorly or wrong.

For example, if you were told by your boss that you need to do better because she was not impressed by your recent performance, you might instead think, "Wow, I do suck. Look at how badly I performed. I'm a bad person".

For people who are experiencing anxiety or depression, it can pretty well be guaranteed that they are also experiencing negative self-statements in their minds.

Often, when you are experiencing anxiety or depression, your self-statements are extremely negative. And you may even repeat them over and over again in your mind as you essentially punish yourself for being "bad".

Studies have shown that negative self-statements are something that we use to attempt to persuade ourselves into behaving better by believing that by placing high pressure against doing something wrong, we can encourage ourselves to change.

Unfortunately, this is not correct, as negative self-statements will not encourage you to change your behavior, but instead may increase your negative behaviors or emotional responses by increasing your internal stress levels.

What you need to do instead is use positive self-statements that encourage you to look beyond your failures and begin seeing the areas in your life where you are doing positive things. In a sense, you want to use these statements to help yourself see "the silver lining" in your behaviors.

Now that you already have a sense of what your biggest problem areas are and what your thoughts are around those problem areas, you can probably identify areas where you may be experiencing negative self-statements.

With clarity around what those statements are, you can begin to consciously and intentionally rewrite those statements to eliminate the stress that you are experiencing in relation to your environmental conditions.

Rewriting these statements will require you to do two things:

First, you need to rewrite the statement intentionally, so that you have something positive to say to yourself when your trigger is being stimulated.

Second, you need to ensure that you are using those statements when your triggers are being stimulated, so that you can begin experiencing the positive benefits of them. Some people call this "using affirmations" because your goal is to affirm your positive self-statements to yourself often enough that your negative self-statements begin to dissolve, and you start genuinely believing the positive self-statements.

At first, you may struggle to believe these self-statements because you are so used to accepting and attaching yourself to the negative self-statements that you have been feeding yourself. As you continue to affirm these new positive self-statements to yourself; however, you will find that you begin to believe them and feel better about yourself.

The best way to get started in writing positive self-statements is to sit with your thought log and identify how you can completely flip the script on your negative self-statements that you cling to.

Step 3: Find New Opportunities for Positive Thinking

In addition to rewriting your self-statements, you should also seek out new opportunities for positive thinking even when your trigger has not necessarily been pulled.

Finding new opportunities to think positively in situations that resulted in you feeling tremendously negative can retrain your brain to see things in a more positive light, including those things that brought you anxiety.

These new opportunities should be sought when you are feeling a peaceful or neutral state of mind, so that you can begin adjusting your overall feelings towards your trigger in general. This way, you do not find yourself living in a constant state of discomfort, worry, or alertness as you attempt to remain prepared to respond to the things that bring you anxiety or depression in your life.

For example, let's say that you experience anxiety because a certain coworker of yours is a bully and has repeatedly treated you poorly over the years despite your best efforts to improve the situation and make work conditions better for yourself.

Perhaps you only experience a panic attack after the bullying has begun, but because of that, you find that you are feeling on edge every single time that coworker is scheduled to work the same shift as you.

You might even find yourself on edge every time someone else brings up that coworker's name because you are so anxious about the negative experiences that you have had with this person in the past. As a result, your constant state of mind will be negative and nervous around this person, which will only further increase your anxious responses any time this person bullies you.

Not only will this increase your unwanted emotional responses, but it will also decrease your ability to stand up for yourself and assert your boundaries around this particular person. As a result, the unwanted experience will continue happening no matter what you do.

By finding a new way to think positively around your anxiety experiences and in general you empower your mind to move into a state of rest rather than existing in a chronic state of worry. This way, you are much more likely to manage your emotions in a more meaningful and effective manner that allows you to achieve the results you desire or need from the unwanted experience.

You can do this by intentionally creating time to monitor and adjust your thoughts around the trigger itself, even when you are not actively triggered. As you are thinking about the thoughts around the upsetting experience, consider what your ideas sound like and begin rewriting them.

Step 4: Implement a Daily Visualization Practice

Another powerful tool that is commonly used in CBT is visualization, as it helps you to see yourself behaving differently from how you normally behave in your life.

With visualization, you can see your triggering experiences and then intentionally observe yourself responding to those triggering experiences more positively and consciously. Visualizing yourself behaving differently has been proven to teach your brain how to react differently in situations that resulted in you experiencing anxious or depressed triggers.

In one study done at the University of Chicago by Dr. Biasiotto, he discovered that by encouraging basketball players to visualize themselves practicing basketball, they could experience significant improvement in their skills. Dr. Biasiotto discovered through his study that players who practiced playing and those who only visualized their practice and never physically practiced were almost on par for their improvements in their performances.

If visualizing themselves practicing basketball without ever actively practicing their skills can help basketball players improve their abilities, imagine what it can do for you when it comes to enduring your own triggers? Visualization is a powerful aid, and that is exactly why it is such a fundamental part of CBT.

Through visualization, you can begin training your brain to improve the way it responds negative triggers, which can ultimately result in you eliminating those triggers in the long run!

To begin using visualization in your own CBT practice, all you need to do is consider your biggest triggers and spend some time visualizing how you would respond differently if you felt that you had more control in those situations.

For example, maybe you experience depression every time you realize that you are trying to build a business, but you cannot earn any income through your company. Perhaps you are feeling like a failure, and like maybe, being an entrepreneur is not for you because you cannot create any success in your venture, and so you are feeling rather down on yourself

In your visualization, you would then picture yourself handling your setbacks with greater intention and success, so that you can begin earning money through your business.

By visualizing yourself closing sales and easily attracting customers into your business, you can begin changing the way that you approach your business and the confidence that you have in yourself as a business owner.

As a result, you will likely see greater improvements in your company and greater motivation within yourself to create those improvements, rather than feelings of defeat and depression.

You should engage in your visualization practice for at least 10 minutes every single day, as research has shown that 10 minutes is the amount of time that you need to change your entire experience.

Then, close your eyes and visualize your successful ability to navigate challenging experiences for 10 minutes. The more you do this, the more confidence you will feel around this particular area of your life, and the easier you will be able to navigate it successfully in real life.

Step 5: Accept Disappointment and Pain

The last part of CBT is that you will need to learn how you can accept disappointment and pain. Although you will learn more about this within ACT, it is a fundamental part of CBT as well, as this acceptance enables you to realize that you may not ever be able to fully eliminate the trigger that you are facing in your life.

Instead, you may simply need to be willing to accept that it always will be challenging for you to navigate and that you will always need to exert a consistent amount of effort in successfully navigating it.

When you can accept that things may never be great, you can stop holding on to the belief that everything will change and suddenly be easier for you.

For example, if you can accept that your Mom always will be unkind towards you because you decided to drop out of college to travel the world, then her consistent jabs towards you for your decision will no longer hurt so much.

They may still be annoying, and they may still cause you to feel bad, but through acceptance and the implementation of other CBT practices, they will no longer cause you to have such intense emotional responses towards them.

Creating acceptance around the things that you cannot control and acceptance around the feelings of disappointment and pain in and of themselves can create a significant amount of peace within you because you stop trying to run away.

Rather than trying to escape the pain or the stress, you can simply recognize it for what it is and appreciate that it is always going to exist for you. However, because you are no longer trying to escape it, you stop creating unnecessary disappointment and pain in your own life by letting the suffering consume you.

As a result, you can minimize the impact of the trigger and experience significant relief around it altogether.

Chapter 4: Strategies to Change Your Core Belief

Core beliefs are the beliefs you hold about yourself. They can be either negative or positive, but they color every interaction you have with others and how you perceive the world around you. These core beliefs are largely unconscious, but they can be identified through plenty of introspection and self-reflection. These beliefs are typically developed over a long period, typically beginning in childhood or through significant life events. These are typically rigid beliefs. You will react according to them, even going so far as to unconsciously force what is happening around you to fit into the core beliefs while denying or disregarding anything that would contradict it.

For example, someone with depression may look at every negative interaction he has as a sign that he is unworthy of love or worthless to everyone around him. However, he will be virtually blind to every instance of those who care about him going out of their way to show they care, such as sending him a silly text of a meme they say on the internet that they know he will appreciate or having his favorite food delivered to him on his birthday.

These core beliefs can be cognitive distortions or colored by negative automatic thoughts, which are important to understand. Once you know how you feel about yourself, you can decide whether you like how you feel. If you do, you know you are secure with yourself. If you do not, you can begin the steps of cognitive restructuring to alter them.

Identifying Your Core Beliefs

Take some time to reflect on the negative automatic thoughts that you often experience. Are there any patterns or recurring messages that you can identify? If so, you can write them down in the outer ring of the diagram provided here, if you have already worked on recognizing and transforming your automatic thoughts.

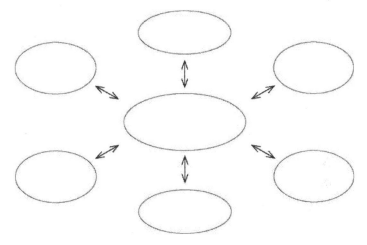

As Esther reflected on her thoughts, she noticed that they all shared a common theme of fear.

As Esther thought about her autc atic thoughts, she noticed a common theme connectir them all: fear. She wrote it in the space provided.

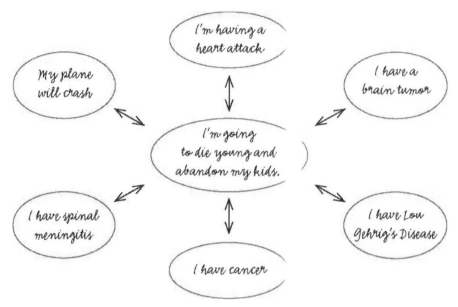

When Esther took a flight, she wa convinced that any turbulence she experienced was n indication of an upcoming crash. It is likely that multiple successful landings would help reduce her fea of flying since they would provide evidence against her apprehension. However, fundamental beliefs tend act as a filter that only allows evidence that back up c r apprehensions.

Every time Esther flew, she wc ld have automatic thoughts such as "We're going dc n!" that made her think she had only just avoided premature death. Instead of feeling secure, she was ertain that her luck might not hold the next time.

Esther found out that core beliefs and automatic thoughts are in a perpetual cycle, where each one is the cause and effect of the other. As you become more aware of your thinking habits, be attentive for moments when your core beliefs are blocking you from seeing the situation objectively. This involves being very aware of the emergence of cognitive distortions in specific situations, and not believing everything your mind is telling you.

It is important to be aware that core negative beliefs can remain unnoticed when we are feeling positive, however they can become more obvious when we experience strong emotions. People who have depression are more likely to have a rise in negative thinking when they are in a bad mood, which increases the risk of having a relapse of depression.

Fortunately, we can train our minds to prevent recurrence, as those who have used cognitive behavioral therapy (CBT) have noticed a decrease in negative ideas when feeling down.

You can also use the downward arrow technique to figure out your basic beliefs. Ask yourself what it would mean if each thought was true at each level. Esther used the downward arrow technique to explore the consequences of her automatic thought related to having cancer: She used the top-down arrow method to look into her core beliefs.

Make a Change of Yourself and Change Your Core Beliefs

Psychology is defined as the study of how our mind works and affects our behavior. Psychology as science investigates the causes of actions and can be used to change practices as well.

Spirituality is different from religion. It is about understanding who you are by looking beyond what we see. Spirituality is very central in forming a person's core beliefs.

The fundamental beliefs of people affect their outward behavior. Through psychology and spirituality, one can transform their lives into what they envision. This can be done through a mindset transformation.

Most of the issues people encounter are a result of having underlying beliefs or questions. Both spirituality and psychology seek to transform your thoughts to improve your life.

To change your life, you must begin by completely transforming your mindset. The nature of your thoughts determines the quality of your life. Positive thoughts, optimism, feelings, and emotions generate some form of energy in your system that allows you to have internal joy.

How we act is a direct manifestation of our thoughts. Psychology and spirituality work together to bring a change in the way a person thinks and generates happiness and fulfillment in our daily lives.

It is possible to change your thoughts and transform your life. Here is a list of ways that you can use to improve your ideas and transform your life positively.

1. Create positive affirmations

Affirmations can also be harmful. Unfortunately, most people are used to making negative affirmations. When a person repeatedly thinks they are going to fail, it is an example of a negative statement. Both negative and positive affirmations affect the functioning of your brain.

Mantras are examples of positive affirmations. Mantras are almost sacred with a spiritual. When creating positive affirmations, they should not be weak or average.

Examples of negative affirmations are: "I can't be able. It is impossible". On the other side, positive affirmations are determined and forceful like "I can or I will". Your brain responds to how you think and, as such, directs the rest of the body organs to act as per your thoughts.

2. Know when to stop

Many people like to dwell on the misfortunes they have encountered along the way. The wrongs they perceive were committed against them by their loved ones. They keep cursing themselves because of the mistakes they made and analyzing what they could have done differently.

It is OK to learn from our past and plan to do better in the future. However, it is not healthy to dwell in the past because we forget to move forward with life.

3. Stop being masochistic

Many times people want to wallow in self-pity and misery. We create self-punishing thoughts and enjoy that state of mind; we focus on pessimistic thoughts and being consistently gloomy. Some people will believe they are naturally unlucky, and so nothing good will ever happen in their lives.

These kinds of thoughts are harmful to your mind and equally detrimental to your physical health.

4. Count your blessings and your joys

Don't take your blessings and joy for granted. Stop grumbling every time you are faced with a challenge. You can counter this by always remembering those that are less fortunate in life than you. It is also possible for a situation to have been worse. Think about that too.

Practice gratitude to enjoy the fullness of life. When you are grateful, the negatives turn to positives. Where there is chaos, the order becomes. Where there is confusion, clarity becomes. This is only possible by having a grateful attitude.

5. Appreciate what you have

The easiest and most excellent way to transform your thoughts is by enjoying and appreciating what you have. Instead of feeling sad because of what you have not achieved in life yet, try being appreciative of where you are now.

Fixing your eyes on more important things is good. However, to reach those great heights, you must begin where you are and enjoy it. If you don't achieve your goals, appreciate what you have so far, and it will motivate you to make more.

6. Enjoy your achievements

Achieving your goals and enjoying them are two different things. Many people set out with goals in mind. As soon as they make them, they become restless and looking for more instead of enjoying what they have achieved. If you aimed to achieve something, follow your goals, and once you do, appreciate the effort and achievement.

7. When trials come, stand tall

It is natural to feel unmotivated and demoralized when we face challenging conditions. We stop moving and focus on exploring the weight of the challenges. However, try and lift your spirits, and you will feel better.

Hold your head high and, with determination, face the challenges to get out of them successfully.

8. Enjoy the child in you

Children are pure in their thinking and innocent. They will fight or quarrel with their friends and forget it so fast and start playing together once again. Unfortunately for grownups, we hold issues within us that poison our spirit and minds. As children, it is essential to practice forgiving and to forget an incident as soon as it has happened and talked over.

9. Seek to be happy and contented

Most people associate their happiness with events in the future. They peg their happiness to future happenings, and if those things don't happen, they are no longer happy. Don't postpone your joy; instead, enjoy your moment today because tomorrow does not belong to you.

10. Control your moods

Don't be a servant to your moods; instead, be the master. Remember, you define your happiness. Never allow circumstances or people to dampen your spirit and make you unhappy.

Other people associate their happiness with material possessions; do not attach your pleasure to things. Choose to be happy, regardless of the situation. Don't allow heartbreaks to dominate; you instead find joy under all circumstances.

11. Resolve to have a happy day

Every day comes with its challenges and situations that can trigger unhappiness. Wake up every day with a determination to be happy. Identify things that bring you joy and focus on those. Look to nature for inspiration and joy. Purpose to stay calm despite the situations you may face and remain happy.

12. Honor your body because it is your temple

Consider your body to be sacred. Keep it well cleaned and avoid dumping garbage, toxic food, and negative thoughts in it. To stay happy, you must stay healthy, both mentally and physically. Engage in active physical exercises often and read inspiring content that acts to motivate you.

13. Learn to meditate daily

Meditation does not have to be complicated, as some people have made it be. Every evening, find a quiet place, focus on how your day was, and pay attention to the good things that made you feel good. If something not so pleasant happened, focus on the lessons you learned from the situation but do not attract negative thoughts by regretting it. By doing this, you fill your mind with gratitude and create a happier you.

14. Forget about changing the world but focus on improving yourself

When people fall short of your expectations, do not get upset. You cannot change the world, but the best way is to change how you view the world by changing yourself. By changing yourself, you allow yourself to adjust to the situations around you, and in so doing, you avoid stress.

15. Use what you have and make the best of it

Do not focus your energies on thinking of what the best could be. Instead, take what you have and make the best out of it. The world is not ideal. Forget the imperfections around you. Change your thoughts and change your world.

Thoughts are compelling. Your ideas can be an obstacle to your happiness or the cause of your mental health issues. You are transforming your thoughts results in the transformation of your mindset. When your mind is changed, you live a healthier, happier, and more fulfilling life.

Cognitive-behavioral therapy focuses on transforming your mindset from a negative one to a positive one. Identifying your core beliefs and how they affect your thought pattern is the beginning of your transformation.

Maintain Mindfulness

There is no way you can acquire a new skill without any guidance or instruction. It would be like being handed the keys to a Ferrari and asked to drive it in busy traffic without ever having done it before - it wouldn't end well. The same is true for mindfulness. If someone just said to you, "go and be mindful" and that was it, then I would have nothing else to say. But don't worry, I'm not going to leave you stranded.

At the heart of Dialectical Behavioral Therapy is the idea of mindfulness. We will examine the various stages of this practice that you need to go through. Simply being aware of its benefits is not enough. It is my aim to give you the skills you need to help yourself.

You may be a bit suspicious about all of this. You may have thought about putting this aside multiple times because it seems unbelievable that learning mindfulness as a skill could be enough to change your life. It's not uncommon for people with BPD to be doubtful of this. How could anyone think that something as basic as mindfulness could help with a problem as complicated as BPD? What does "mindfulness" even mean? Filled with mind? You might think it's some kind of religious thing from Buddhists, so you don't pay it any attention. You can't imagine how your problems could be solved by just breathing, right? These thoughts make sense.

It's understandable to be skeptical and raise an eyebrow when presented with the idea of mindfulness, especially if you are not familiar with what it means or how to start.

Laying the Groundwork

You're probably trying to figure out how often and for how long you should practice being mindful each time. Since you're only just starting, you should begin with just 15 to 20 minutes a day. You can easily split that up into two sessions, once at the start of your day and once at the end.

As you get used to your practice, you could begin to add a bit of time to your sessions each day. We're going to cover ways in which you can be mindful all through your day. Still, we're also going to cover the basics of picking a set time each day for a more focused, formal session. This is important because being deliberate about it is the only way you can be mindful. One more thing, I ought to mention is that no matter how good you become aware of yourself, you must make sure you keep up your practice day after day.

This is not a prerequisite. Find a time that is convenient for you and commit to it. If you find that you're exhausted at the end of your day, then you definitely would be better off practicing in the afternoon or the morning. If you have to start your mornings early and have a lot to do to prepare your family for the day, you might want to consider noon or night for practice. It's all up to you. The point is that you must make it a habit, and remember the only way habits are formed constant repetition. Do what you need to make it happen. Leave yourself a note somewhere you'll always pass by, remember, or set a reminder on your phone.

If it's a seated mindfulness practice, then it would be best to adopt a posture where your chest is open, meaning you keep your arms away from your chest. You also want to make sure that your bottom is firmly and evenly planted on the seat. Choose a good chai, which allows you to sit up comfortably. If you need a few pillows to support your back, then use them. Make sure your feet are flat on the floor, firmly and evenly. Do not cross your ankles or your legs. Your shoulders must be back and upright. Don't hunch over. You may keep your arms on your lap. If you like, you can turn your palms upwards. A considerable part of this mindfulness practice is also aware of your posture as you sit. Now that you know how to sit, you're going to practice while keeping your eyes open.

Owning Your Mind

The more you practice mindfulness, the more you'll find that you own your mind. You are more in control of it. Right now, I can see how you'd think this is an impossible feat. However, it's true! As you practice, you will discover you are not your emotions or your thoughts, but something more.

For the most part, people tend to ignore how much of a habit thought patterns are. We never really think about our thinking because we weren't taught how to do that. This is where mindfulness can help again. If your mind is not trained, it can cause you a lot of pain and heartache without you even being aware of it. Like a pendulum, you swing from one extreme to the other. You either get so enmeshed in your mind that you pay way too much attention to specific thoughts or worry about the point of obsession and are unable to see past your nose. Either way, you don't pay attention to your thinking habits. It almost seems to you that things tend to unfold on their own, and you have no power over how you react. I don't need to tell you how being on one extreme or the other can cause you issues and suffering. Mindfulness will help you grow in curiosity, awareness, and attention. This is how you'll finally own your mind and break the habits of thought you've got.

The Need for Curiosity and Attentiveness

When you don't develop your attention, and when you're not curious about life, you'll be stuck in your usual routines. Routines may help you avoid the pain you feel, but in the end, they also keep you stuck, and this can add to more pain in the end. It's never worth trying to ignore your emotions and thoughts.

You have to pay attention to your thoughts. This means you need to pause now and then and take an unbiased look at your mind. How fast or slow are you thinking? Are your thoughts a jumbled mess or well put together? Are they loving and kind or angry and resentful? What exactly is it that you're thinking about?

The point of mindfulness is to take charge of your mind and thought processes, and by extension, your emotions. As you pay attention, the peace and serenity you feel in your life will go up a hundredfold. It might be difficult to believe that mindfulness can help you achieve all this, especially as you've never done it before, but I promise you it works.

The Practice

As you practice, pay attention to how your body and mind feel. This will help you learn all the things you can do to decrease your suffering through your emotions and thoughts. In the DBT space, these actions are known as the "what" and "how" skills — "what" being the actions you take to be mindful, and "how" being the way you go about it.

Try the practices that you will be given in this at least one time. You'll need a journal so that you can take down notes on your experiences after each practice. You will find that some of the practices feel better for you than others. However, don't stick to them just yet without trying everything so that you can tell what works for you and what doesn't. The goal isn't to get you to like the practice but to encourage you to become more curious and give your mind a challenge.

One more thing I should mention is that your mind will wander. You must be comfortable with that fact. When you notice your mind has gone off on a tangent, do not beat up on yourself. Noticing is progress! So simply bring your mind back to your mindful task, whatever it may be. Each time your mind wanders, and you bring it back, you will get better at maintaining mindfulness. Remember, your mind is like a muscle. This is how it gets stronger.

The Power of Intention

You cannot practice mindfulness without intention. The intention is a beautiful thing because if you can do something mindlessly, then with it, you can do it mindfully. Intention means you're choosing to pay attention to something with a specific goal in mind. Therefore, you could brush your teeth like always, while your thoughts are on autopilot, wondering about bills and mortgages, or you can spend that time noticing the way you brush, the way your mouth feels, and so on. You notice the desire to think about how to take care of the bills, but then you shift your attention back to the simple act of brushing your teeth. As you brush, your mind will wander off. When it does, you can simply come back to brushing. You can do this with any activity that you do on the regular, whether it's driving, walking, doing the dishes, or laundry. This is how you infuse mindfulness into your daily activities.

There is a misconception that the goal of mindfulness is to have a mind that never wanders. That's impossible. You will always have thoughts in your head. That's the function of your brain. What mindfulness is, is intentionally choosing to refocus your attention back on the tasks at hand each time your mind wanders. It's not about keeping your mind quiet and empty.

Decide, Commit, Succeed

As you decide to practice being mindful, you've got to keep reminding yourself of what you've set out to do and why. It matters that in the beginning, you are clear about the fact that you're going to be mindful of the task you've chosen, whether it's doing the dishes or washing your car. Tell yourself you will do this mindfully, and automatically your brain takes a cue that it needs to focus on the task before you. Once you commit this way, you are more likely to succeed.

A Different Practice for Each Day

All you need to do is intend to change at least one of the things you do habitually for every day, just for a week. Try getting out on the right if you're used to getting out of bed on the left side. Do you usually open doors with your dominant hand? Commit to using the other hand. It's all about doing something different for a set period and paying full attention to the process.

Chapter 5: Strategies to Develop a Positive Mindset

Identify Your Goals

Goals are the way in which we set targets for ourselves of things we want to achieve. If we live a life without any plans, we may feel that we have not achieved anything. We might feel discouraged or even hopeless. When starting to set goals for ourselves, we must first establish a time frame and have some idea of how to execute it. Goals also offer a sense of purpose and a way to measure our success and our ourselves. If you set a large goal for yourself, it is wise to set smaller goals to help you achieve it over time, and it enables you to measure your progress towards accomplishing the larger goal. Those smaller subtasks are also a great way to avoid procrastination because setting purposes makes you accountable. They are constant reminders we cannot avoid what we have promised ourselves that we would achieve. How do you become successful, and how do you achieve direction in life?

Finding Your Vision

Your vision is one of the most important things you need to have if you hope to grow and want to become successful. The purpose of a vision is to act as your WHY.

The purpose of a vision is to inspire and fill you with energy and life. It should help guide you, lead you forward, and give you a sense of energy and drive. Your vision should be connected to your core values, and your motivations should be clear to yourself. A mission will also give you a direction in a world that's filled with different kinds of choices. It will help narrow your focus; it will help you eliminate those things that are external or irrelevant. When you are seeking to identify your vision, you should sit down in a quiet place and consider all of your options and what your goals are. Much like searching for your core beliefs, you will find yourself thinking about the things that will make you happy and successful. When you come up with these goals, you must make sure that you consider the following:

- **Unique** - Is your goal unique? Does it match your plans and your passions? Can you imagine yourself feeling this individual role?
- **Simple vision** - Your vision should be simple, clear, and you should be able to explain it easily. You will need others to help you achieve it, so they need to be able to understand, believe, and follow your vision as well.
- **Focused Vision** - Your vision should be precise and targeted. It should not be too broad.
- **Be bold** - A vision should be courageous, and it should be large enough to be worthy of your abilities and your skills.
- **Beneficial** - A good vision will have a purpose, and it should benefit others, not just yourself.

- **Aligned** - A division should be aligned with your objectives, and you should be able to understand how you will achieve it as well as explain the process to others.
- **Inspiring** - Express your vision in a way that is inspiring; you must attract a team, and they must be willing to follow because they have become inspiring as well.
- **Engaging** - Your vision should arouse curiosity among your team.
- **Making your goals achievable** - If you want to accomplish anything by then, making your goals doable is crucial.

People who do not have goals tend to have no direction, and they tend to let life happen to them. Setting goals allows you to have a measure of control over your life. When you take charge, you are both able to enjoy it and also know where you are headed.

How to Set Your Goals

Make sure your goals and your purposes are aligned.

Sometimes you may have goals, but you do not feel motivated to achieve them. Perhaps these goals seem attractive and accomplishable, but you don't have any motivation. The problem, in this case, is that your goals are not aligned. There are two ways you can set goals. The first is very traditional in that you set goals based on what you think you should do or what you think others think you should do. These kinds of goals can be achievable, of course, and they do work somewhat, but they are not the kind of goals that you will stick to long-term because they don't match your sense of purpose. If you do achieve them, you may not have any particular feeling of success, even though you may have expected one because this was not a goal that was aligned to your purpose.

When you're setting goals, it's very important to focus on what is inside you, on what you want, your desires, your passions, or your dreams. Whether or not the goal is achievable is not the first important thing; the first thing to build is a goal that is goals that are aligned with your heart and your soul. Once you understand that these exist and you have figured out what they are, then you will be able to decide how to make them practical and achievable.

Your Goals Need To Be Seen

Simply knowing what you want is not actually enough; you also need to write everything down and plan for how you're going to achieve it. You also should check this paper often, come back and look at your goal, and use it to stay focused.

Try To Have a Partner to Keep You Accountable

Goals are designed to be achieved, and the chance of them being achieved is increased when they're connected to your sense of purpose. When you share goals with someone, else you will find they will help you stay focused.

Identify Your Worthwhile Goals

What this means is that you must make sure that what you want to do is worth doing. If you are challenged and find things in your, way if the goal is not worth, doing you will lose motivation.

Don't Be Afraid Of Obstacles

Things will get in your way; expect this. There will be obstacles and roadblocks up ahead; you need to be able to anticipate and deal with them as they come. Don't get discouraged. Simply be prepared.

Don't Procrastinate

Don't avoid the unpleasant tasks ahead of you. You have things you have to get done, they may not be nice things, but you need to do them anyway. There are many reasons why people procrastinate:

They may find that the task does not suit them and they want to do something else. Very few people in the world want to change their ways that take up hard jobs. They would rather stay with what they know.

If a person is ignorant or lacks the knowledge to complete a task, they will try to avoid it. Frankly most would rather avoid a job entirely than risk the chance of feeling embarrassed or being asked to put a lot into it.

Avoid perfectionists, as they tend to be procrastinators. If they feel, they have nothing to learn, they won't take risks.

Learning new ways and behaviors is not always a pleasant thing. However, avoiding change and procrastinating is not going to help you achieve your goal. Once you have found the way to get to your goal and know the changes that you must make to gain it, you must learn to avoid procrastination.

- **Set up a reward system** - Make sure you have something in place to reward you for when you achieve some of your smaller goals. You will find that facing negative tasks will be easier if there is a reward at the end of it.
- **Re-engage** - Don't be afraid if a task seems hard. Simply break it into smaller subtasks and then re-approach it. Go back to it every day or as often as possible in order to deal with these unpleasant things. If you do it often, you will find that you will become familiar with it will not seem so bad, and you will get it done.
- **Take notes and keep a list** - Write things down to make sure that you know what needs to get done. Think about it often and check it every day. Stay on top of these things because this is a surefire way to get your goals accomplished because you will constantly be checking in on and doing what needs to be done.
- **Be accountable to someone** - If you try to do it all alone, you may find it hard going. Seek someone who can hold you accountable for what needs to be done. It will make the task go faster and easier.

- **Ask yourself what?** - What would happen if you put the task off? This question may persuade you to do it faster.
- **Dream big** - Don't forget to imagine what will happen once you achieve your goals. Anticipate that feeling of satisfaction. You know you want to change things in your life, and maybe you keep putting it off, but if you remember the feeling of getting it done and achieving your goal will feel great, then you will do it.

Stop Arguing With Yourself Just Do It. Once You Start, It Always Gets Easier

Imagine the disappointment of how you would feel if you didn't accomplish your goal and let that fear motivate you. You want to make your life better, don't you? So, don't put it off. Start now. What you have now is not what you want. Imagine knowing that you have accomplished what you set out to do.

Chapter 6: Strategies to Learn How to Practice CBT with Your Everyday Life

Sleep Tight

Problems with the quality of sleep appear both as a result of having anxiety and depression as well as causes in early childhood. Depression and anxiety affect sleep in numerous ways that most often go undetected until they become problematic. Lack of ability to fall asleep and stay asleep, nightmares, sleep paralysis, and difficulty getting out of bed as a result of poor sleep quality are the most common sleep problems among those suffering from depression. While a lack of quality of sleep may slow down your progress, you should do the best you can to address this problem and make sure you are getting as much rest as you need.

Here are what you can do to improve your sleep:

- **Try to follow a sleep schedule**

Think about your daily routine and the most desirable time to go to bed and wake up. Come up with an ideal plan for going to bed and getting up. If you're having trouble falling asleep, you may have difficulty sleeping according to your schedule. This shouldn't alarm you because your program aims at building a healthy habit instead of being instantly effective. Here are a number of ways for you to practice your sleep schedule:

- ## Don't force yourself to fall asleep

Understand that whether or not you will fall asleep is out of your control. Acknowledge that you can't force yourself to fall asleep. Trust your body's sleep cycle, and acknowledge that you will fall asleep when your body and mind feel ready to fall asleep.

- ## Be consistent with the time that you wake up every morning

Regardless of whether or not you managed to fall asleep the previous night, be persistent in getting up every morning around the same time. If this is difficult for you, one of the ways to motivate yourself to get up in the morning is to have scheduled activities. Knowing that you have to be somewhere at a particular time will further motivate you to get off your bed even if you don't feel like it.

- ## Take sleep seriously

Avoid napping during the day or using your bedroom and bed for activities other than sleep. What you are attempting is to get your body and mind adjusted to associate your bed with sleep and nothing else.

- ## Change your way of thinking about sleep

While acknowledging that your sleep problems result from ongoing health issues, avoid trying to force yourself to fall asleep in any way, shape, or form. Ironically, the less you worry about sleep, the more you will be likely actually to fall asleep and stay asleep. While it is alright for you to research sleep problems and get educated on the topic, don't turn your efforts into an obsession. The more anxiety present around sleep, the more difficult it will be for you to relax and fall asleep.

Healthy Sleeping Habits

While there is no quick fix with insomnia in depression and anxiety, there are numerous common-sense tips to upsurge your chances of healthy sleep and overall well-being. Here's what you can do to enhance healthy sleep:

Reduce Screen Time

At the very minimum, reduce or completely eliminate the use of electronics a couple of hours before going to bed. Preferably, reduce the use of TV, computers, and other devices when it's not necessary.

Practice mindfulness and meditation

Think of mindfulness as an umbrella term for many calming activities you can do to relax your mind, quiet your thoughts, and unwind before going to bed. These calming activities include a broad choice of activities such as journaling, prayer, Qi Gong exercises, yoga, meditation, as well as light homeopathic remedies that have a beneficial impact on your nervous system.

Healthy Eating

One of your primary goals with recovery from depression and anxiety will be to improve your diet. The diet has a great effect on your mental health since nutrient deficiency can cause hormonal imbalances and affect your mood. One of the major hindrances to establishing a healthy diet with depression is the lack of strength and the ability to plan. If it feels hard to move around, you will have a more difficult time planning grocery shopping and choosing your groceries in a way that is beneficial to your diet. Planning your diet, following your diet schedule, and being careful about the food you choose is very important for you to feel the beneficial effects within the optimal time frame.

Healthy foods can alleviate some of your symptoms in numerous ways. Foods that are known to be antioxidants and anti-inflammatory, as well as contain omega-3 fats, can have an impact on your overall mood. On the other hand, too many carbohydrates and fast food may cause insulin spikes in your blood that could make you drowsy, sleepy, irritable, and nervous.

How to Set Healthy Diet Goals and Stick to Them

To stay effective with improving your diet, it is important to establish a schedule that is attainable, realistic, and achievable. While there is plenty you can learn about beneficial diet plans and routines that will promote good mental health, make sure to account for your ability to follow through. If your lifestyle resources can't support the idea of the perfect diet, plan for an optimally healthy diet. Here's how to plan your diet to support your recovery from anxiety and depression:

Prioritize Improvements

It is most likely that not all of your diet habits are bad, but you need to improve some of the aspects instead. A healthy diet is not only made out of healthy food choices, but also an appropriate schedule and a good measure of satisfying and healthy. Remember that you also need to feel good about the foods you eat in order to stay motivated.

Plan Grocery Shopping and Budgeting

Grocery planning and creating a smart food budget is challenging for most people, mainly because it requires setting time out of your busy schedule to think about grocery shopping and the amounts of money available for it. To follow through with a healthy schedule, you will need to make sure that you always have a sufficient supply of healthy foods. With your preferred diet plan in mind, create a grocery shopping schedule and budget that will include dates and times you will go grocery shopping as well as the amount of money you will spend.

Create an Eating Schedule

Plan your meals in detail. List all of your meals, including the times you will eat. Do the best you can to stay diligent and follow through with the schedule, even if it means pre-making meals and taking them with you.

Create a Meal Preparation Schedule

Healthy meals are easy, simple, fast, delicious, and homemade. To avoid temptations to snack, plan for the best time to prepare your meals. You may have to get your meal ready the day before, or the night before, if you have time to make them throughout the day.

Physical Activity

Regular physical activity can greatly improve your mood and help relieve symptoms of depression and anxiety. One of the obstacles to establishing a good exercise routine is the ever-present tiredness that is typical for depression. Working around your symptoms and objective limitations when creating your exercise goals is important to have attainable, realistic, and practical routines that you will be able to manage in the long run.

Why Is Exercise Important To Recover From Depression And Anxiety?

The best exercises are the ones that you feel are manageable and you're certain to be able to follow through with. Depression can have an isolating impact, driving you into solitude. Exercising alongside a friendly group can have a stimulating effect.

Physical Effects on Mental Health

Exercise is proven to cause beneficial changes in your brain, such as activity patterns with a calming effect, anti-inflammatory effects, and neural growth. The endorphin release during physical activity has a grounding effect on your body, regulating breathing and shifting focus from your thoughts to physical experiences.

Confidence Improvement

Exercise improves confidence in the end. No matter what the impact it may have, on your weight and shape, the demonstrated ability of regular exercise will assure you of positive personality traits, like diligence, discipline, and competence.

Achievement and Satisfaction

Tracking and completing exercise goals will bring a sense of achievement and satisfaction with your abilities and performance. With gradual progress from simple to more demanding fitness goals, you will build up not only confidence but also your faith in the capacity to grow and change. Over time, your belief in your capacity will strengthen, and you will assure yourself of your strength. Even small positives like being able to show up on time, sticking through the entire exercise regardless of the initial inconveniences, and beating shyness have the potential to build up a strong positive self-image.

Help and Emotional Support

In the same way you need to support your body throughout the process of recovery, your mind and feelings also need care and love. Being self-sufficient is a virtue, but going through depression alone, without the support of friends and family is unnecessarily burdening. Overcoming the desire to appear strong and independent might feel uncomfortable. Perhaps, you don't like to rely on others for help. But, breaking the barrier between you and your social environment is best done through the acceptance of help and care. Your support system, which may include friends and family, can lift a lot of weight off your shoulders and give you the necessary love and acceptance you need. Here's what your friends and family can help you with to support your recovery:

Socializing and Outdoor Activities

Doing activities to get fresh air is beneficial for both physical and mental health, as well as connecting and socializing. Isolation is common for those who suffer from depression, and you should work to overcome the urge to be alone, even if, most of the time, you want to be alone. However, schedule social activities and follow through with them regardless of whether or not you feel motivated to do so. Being more socially active is likely to be a part of your recovery plan, as well as one of the activities you can practice with behavioral activation.

Conversation and Understanding

Opening up about the dark thoughts and feelings may seem difficult, but it will help you get the support you need. The problems will likely sound less dramatic than envisioned in your mind once you simply talk about them. The exaggerated thinking typical of depression is causing you to magnify everything from difficulties to feelings, fears, and doubts. Talking will help overcome many things that are bothering you, and bonding and receiving encouragement will enforce the positive beliefs you're looking to create.

Encouragement and Motivation

Aside from having someone to keep you company, you need to surround yourself with people who are willing to motivate you and lift your spirits. Those should be the people you feel comfortable talking to at any time and on any topic, because they are always ready to support you. Your therapist will be among those who are supportive, but make sure to open up to as many people as you trust. You'll benefit from hearing others' positive thoughts about yourself.

Spirituality

Oftentimes, spirituality is confused with organized religion. However, they are not one and the same. Every person has an inborn spiritual sense and inclination, which has nothing to do with expressing certain opinions, following a person wearing special clothing, or reading a certain book. Spirituality is our instinctive curiosity about our roots, our need to investigate, think about, and contemplate the purpose of it all, and our capability and willingness to go beyond the physical world and our material desires in pursuit of something that feels more significant.

Even if you don't consider yourself a person of faith, your relationship to the world around you and the depth of your understanding of life can be just as meaningful.

No matter what one's beliefs or lack thereof may be, spirituality can bring about feelings of admiration. Many famous thinkers, scientists, and artists who did not think of themselves as religious devoted their lives to

86

comprehending the world and human life, and were deeply moved by the process. Even without religious faith, forming a relationship with the environment and gaining a deeper understanding of life can be a significant experience.

Take a few moments each day to contemplate the incredible things that make up our reality. The remarkable human capacity for love. The intricate and varied yet biologically unified character of life. The astonishing fact that life exists whatsoever! The boundless scope of the cosmos and the relative smallness of Earth.

Humans possess the capacity to think in an abstract manner, create art, and recognize beauty. It has been established that there are more bacteria than human cells in the body, and these bacteria are essential for our wellbeing. Additionally, 96 percent of the universe is composed of dark matter, which remains mysterious and largely unknown.

The incredible power of stories that were crafted thousands of years ago to still evoke our laughter and tears is remarkable. Take a moment to reflect on what it is that truly amazes you.

For those who follow a certain set of beliefs, many of the teachings can be inspiring. The great thing about Buddhism, philosophical Taoism, and certain sects of other religions is that they provide inspiring ideas, introspection and insight to people of all beliefs and backgrounds. Spirituality is a very personal matter, so it is up to you to find verses from religious texts, commentaries, rituals, or sermons that are inspiring. If you practice a faith that has meaning for you, we encourage you to search for deeper wisdom or spiritual experiences. Look for a scholar, teacher, priest, imam, or minister that you respect, and ask them for advice on how to explore your faith.

Chapter 7: Emotional Intelligence and CBT

Emotional intelligence by definition tells us that it is the capacity to control, to be understanding of, and to be able to express yourself. It is also the ability to handle interpersonal relationships both emphatically and judiciously. There are five different components to emotional intelligence. The five components of EQ are:

- Regulation of yourself

- Awareness of yourself

- Empathy

- Motivation

- Social skills

The use of emotional intelligence is simply to help you lead a more fulfilling life with less turbulence and emotional turmoil. From such a life, many other benefits will inevitably arise, concerning everything from your relationships to professional success to overall happiness.

Emotional intelligent people are usually better at adapting to dynamic environments, handling stress, and working in teams. Right away, you can probably think of quite a few life scenarios or vocations where emotional intelligence can be very useful. In fact, emotional intelligence is the very core of success and has been for a long time before psychologists assigned a name to the skill in some careers. In various managerial positions, for example, emotional intelligence is all but a prerequisite. Then there are professions that not only revolve around working with people but helping them, sometimes in life-threatening situations and periods of crisis. Social workers, nurses, therapists, and many other similar professionals rely heavily on their own emotional intelligence, as they would otherwise not be very good at their jobs. Apart from work, emotional intelligence is incredibly important in dealing with many personal problems as well.

Emotional intelligence can also have an indirect but profound effect on our physical health. It has long been common knowledge that chronic emotional turmoil brought on by things like stress, depression, anxiety, and suppressed anger can lead to the early onset of a wide range of serious health complications. Cardiovascular issues, diabetes, a diminishing immune system, and even various forms of cancer can all be facilitated by prolonged stress. Emotional intelligence is what helps us deal with our emotional baggage efficiently and holistically, which rids us of things like stress, so the positive link is quite clear.

Emotional intelligence also helps with mental health. There are many cases of severe mental health deterioration resulting not from genetics or brain damage but from an inability to cope with life and its many emotional trials. This is especially true for traumatic experiences that many people can't deal with, but our mental health can also suffer over a prolonged period of repressing our feelings and bottling everything up. Whether it's about avoiding to solve a problem or a simple lack of awareness, many folks, unfortunately, end up repressing their feelings and piling up the baggage throughout their lives. Eventually, living like this can eventually lead to a nervous breakdown.

Emotional intelligence helps us avoid these situations and rid ourselves of that baggage by understanding our emotions, categorizing them, and healthily processing them. On top of that, emotionally intelligent people tend to simply be tougher. As such, not only are they better at processing their emotions, but they simply have a higher resistance to negative events and various stresses in life. In that regard, emotional intelligence can also be viewed as a sort of shield or improved immunity. That certainly doesn't mean that emotionally intelligent people don't feel anything when they are beset by an unfortunate event or a tragedy, far from it. They will feel as can be expected, but the difference is in how they process the emotional input. As such, it isn't so much that emotionally intelligent individuals are impervious as it is that they are good at picking up the pieces and getting back on their path as soon as possible.

Emotionally intelligent individuals are also less prone to blow things out of proportion both before and after the fact, which further reduces their stress levels. For instance, many people might stress over upcoming professional or personal events and completely give into uncontrolled panic. Not only does this hinder our mental health, but it also negatively impacts performance.

Emotional intelligence helps us keep our emotions at bay while looking at potential situations objectively, which usually makes them much less scary. After all, a lot of our daily stress comes from things that haven't even happened yet or might not happen at all.

A high emotional intelligence also gives us clarity of mind, which is important in making all sorts of decisions, for instance. Unorganized minds tend to have a lot of noise and emotional clutter, which can interfere with a person's ability to analyze the situation objectively, weigh their options, and choose the best course. Things like anxiety can completely cloud our judgment at times or outright cripple our thinking process, which is a problem that emotionally intelligent people don't suffer from.

Emotionally intelligent people are also generally more confident in their hunches and gut feelings, which often come from an unconscious analysis of reality. In fact, the real beauty of emotional intelligence is that people who possess it are very adept at balancing their objectivity with their own, subjective emotions. To put it simply, emotional intelligence reduces the risk of our feelings infringing on our ability to think rationally and observe reality with an objective view.

Because they understand their feelings and the causes of those feelings so well, high emotional intelligent individuals can use those emotions as an extension of the information they gather through their observations. It is, therefore, hardly surprising that studies have found nurses and other healthcare professionals to perform better at their jobs if their emotional intelligence was determined to be high.

Chapter 8: Overthinking and CBT

Overthinking happens when the brain becomes too caught up with certain thoughts, thus causing the person to fail in acting upon the said thoughts. It is essentially a mental state wherein the brain is trapped in a cycle of repeated analysis over the same topic or issue.

As a result, energy is expended unnecessarily, while signs of mental strain begin manifesting in the individual's day-to-day activities and even in one's interactions with other people.

To demonstrate better how the brain works when it is engaged in overthinking, go through the following list of scenarios—some of which may even sound familiar to you:

- You cannot stop thinking about a personal problem or an event that has already transpired. Rather than focus on how to solve your current predicament, you cannot seem to pull yourself away from these thoughts. No matter what you do, your thoughts keep coming back to the problem or the event itself—not what you can do to get yourself out of this situation.

- Something terrible has happened to you. As a result, you cannot seem to stop asking yourself why that has happened to you. You also find yourself ruminating about what would have happened

94

instead if only you had done things a little differently.

- Your mind jumps to the worst conclusions, even without any solid or sound basis at all. It has been occurring to your regularly so that, by now, the negative thoughts appear to be following some sort of pattern in your head.

- You find yourself obsessing about the tiny details in your day-to-day experiences, especially when it involves interacting with those around you.

- You even come up with dialogues in your head, recreating mentally certain life events where you think you could have done better.

- You assign meaning to every word, thought, and action that sometimes goes beyond what is reasonable and realistic. People also say that you read into things, only to realize later on that they are not worth your time and effort.

If you recognize yourself in any of these scenarios, and if you think that such scenarios happen to you frequently, then you might be falling into the habit of overthinking.

As shown in the examples above, addressing this issue is of the utmost importance. Overthinking is keeping you from moving forward and experiencing new things in life. It is like having your hand tied with a rope that is attached to a pole. You can only go around in circles around the same thing, over and over again.

What Overthinking Is and Isn't?

Right off the bat, it should be made clear that overthinking is not a form of mental illness. It is, however, a common symptom that can be observed among different types of anxiety disorders.

For example, Ben has been diagnosed with panic disorder. He is prone to overthink about when the next panic attack might happen. If he thinks something might trigger an attack, he cannot help himself but obsess over this possibility. As such, his tendency to overthink these triggers only serves to increase the risk of panic attacks.

You do not have to be suffering from an anxiety disorder to engage in overthinking. This is an all-too-common human experience that happens almost naturally to everyone.

You may feel concerned about what you have said to your friend the last time you talked over the phone. Perhaps, you are worried about an upcoming test or job interview. You might feel a little too conscious about how others perceive you at work. These are just some examples of common scenarios where overthinking is at play.

It should also be noted that there is a distinction between the two forms of overthinking:

- **Brooding over the past**

Dwelling about the mistakes you have done, and the opportunities you have missed out on can be detrimental to your current happiness and mental state.

- **Worrying about the future**

The uncertainty of what will happen next can trap a person into a never-ending cycle of "what-ifs" and "should-Is."

Overthinking is also different from introspection. The latter involves gaining personal insights and fresh personal perspectives about a certain matter. You introspect with a clear purpose in mind.

Overthinking, on the other hand, involves negative feelings about things that are usually outside of your control. As such, you will not feel like you have progressed at all after engaging in overthinking.

Causes of Overthinking

There is no single origin or trigger for one to engage in overthinking. It can be born out of genuine worry for one's welfare and those of others. Some overthink as a result of how they have been conditioned to think by their parents, their teachers, and their peers.

Extreme forms of overthinking are believed to be rooted in certain mental and psychological issues that a person is suffering from. These include but are not limited to:

- post-traumatic stress disorder (PTSD);

- panic disorder;

- social anxiety disorder;

- substance-induced anxiety disorder;

- separation anxiety disorder;

- different types of phobias, particularly agoraphobia;

- physical, mental, and/or emotional trauma.

Linking mental health issues with overthinking, however, is not as straightforward as it may seem. Some experts suggest that overthinking contributes to the decline of one's mental health. However, others are reporting that existing mental health problems can trigger a person to engage in overthinking.

Giving a definitive answer on the actual cause of overthinking, therefore, can get you stuck in a loop. The actual case may also vary from one individual to another.

Rather than ruminate over the exact origin of overthinking, you should focus instead on learning how to assess yourself for signs of overthinking. Through this, you will be able to check if your tendency to overthink is getting out of hand already.

Signs You Are Being Controlled by Overthinking

Much like any human behavior, the effects of overthinking can be described as a dichotomy.

On one end, overthinking may be considered helpful since it allows a person to learn from past experiences and prevent the recurrence of certain mistakes in the future. When used in this way, overthinking can be beneficial in terms of problem solving and decision-making.

The problem begins when these thoughts become excessive, thus creating anxiety, stress, and a sense of fear and dread within the person. At this point, overthinking has gone beyond simply thinking too much about a person or a thing — overthinking has become an obsession that disrupts an individual's capacity to function and interact with other people.

If you are experiencing at least one of the following situations, then it's evident that you are being controlled by overthinking:

- Continually measuring your worth, success, and happiness against the people around you;

- Focusing on the worst possible outcomes whenever you or someone you care for is involved in something risky or dangerous;

- Having trouble in keeping up with and contributing to conversations because you go over your potential responses for too long that either you

99

miss the appropriate timing for your responses, or the conversation itself has already ended;

- Worrying about future activities and task that you must accomplish so much that you feel overwhelmed at just the thought of having to do any of them;

- Repeatedly thinking about personal mistakes and failures from the past, thus preventing you from moving on with your life;

- Repeatedly reliving past trauma, loss, or abusive situation that robs you of your chance to cope with it;

- Failing to calm down your racing thoughts and overwhelming but vague emotions that seemingly manifest out of nowhere.

Please note that the signs of overthinking, as highlighted above, are not exhaustive. However, if you find yourself continuously thinking about certain aspects of your life, or you find yourself in an endless cycle of non-productive thoughts, then that in itself is a sign that you are embroiled in overthinking.

Effects of Overthinking on You

No matter how similar the circumstances are between two people, their respective manner of overthinking would not be the same. As such, each individual would feel the effects of overthinking differently.

It has been observed by psychologists, however, that those who cannot control their tendency to overthink suffer from a decreased quality of life. To give you a background on the possible effects of overthinking in your life, here are some common examples of difficulties faced by those who have been identified as chronic over-thinkers:

- Making new friends or keeping the ones they already have can be tough due to their struggles in effectively communicating their thoughts and feelings.

- They find it hard to go out and have fun doing their hobbies because they have already spent their time and energy ruminating about certain matters inside their heads.

- Setting up appointments or even simply going to the store can be an arduous task for them.

- Taking and exercising full control of their thoughts and emotions seem impossible because their mind is already strained and overworked.

Looking through these points, you can surmise that overthinking can ruin your relationships, isolate you from the rest of the world, and it can increase your risk of developing other serious mental issues, such as depression and anxiety disorder.

The bottom line is that overthinking has far-reaching effects on almost everything you do and want to do in life. It does not only impose limits on you but also on those who wish to express their support to you. This means that overthinking can create serious problems not only in your personal abilities but also in the kind of relationships that you will have.

Currently, there is no single form of treatment that you can adopt to completely relieve yourself of overthinking and its negative effects on you. Perhaps, one day, the mental health community would be able to come up with the ultimate solution for this.

However, this should not stop you from seeking out methods that can help you control your thoughts and eliminate your tendency to overthink. This book shall help you understand and apply the strategies that would work best for you, given the peculiarity of your situation.

Keeping a Thought Journal

Journaling can be used in two ways to help you when it comes to CBT. The first way is through simply journaling in a brain-dump format where you write down everything you are thinking about and all of the thoughts and feelings you are having so that you can get them out of your mind. The more you can write about when you are engaging in this type of journaling, the more you are getting out of your mind, and therefore the better you are going to feel. This can be incredibly helpful in supporting you with overcoming any form of anxiety that you may be dealing with as it allows you to get your worries out of your mind and let them go.

The other type of journaling that you can do that will be both supportive of helping you get things off your mind while also allowing you to organize your thoughts and track your experiences is called dysfunctional thought journaling. Some people also call this keeping a dysfunctional thought record.

Your dysfunctional thought record should have seven columns drawn onto a piece of paper so that you can write down seven pieces of information each time you have a dysfunctional thought. In the first column on the far left, you want to write down the time and date of your dysfunctional thought. In the second, you want to write down what the situation was that lead to the dysfunctional thought. Write about this part in detail. In the third column, write about the automatic thought you had immediately after the situation transpired. In the fourth column, write about any emotions you experienced as a result of the situation and your automatic thought. In the fifth column, write down the dysfunctional thought itself. In the sixth column, write down alternative thoughts that you could think that would serve as a more positive and helpful alternative to the initial thought you had. In the seventh column, write down the outcome of the exercise, or how it has helped you confront the negative thought. If the process of confronting and addressing the thought helped you feel better or change your belief, or at least decrease your troubling emotions, write that down, too. The more you can keep track of, the better.

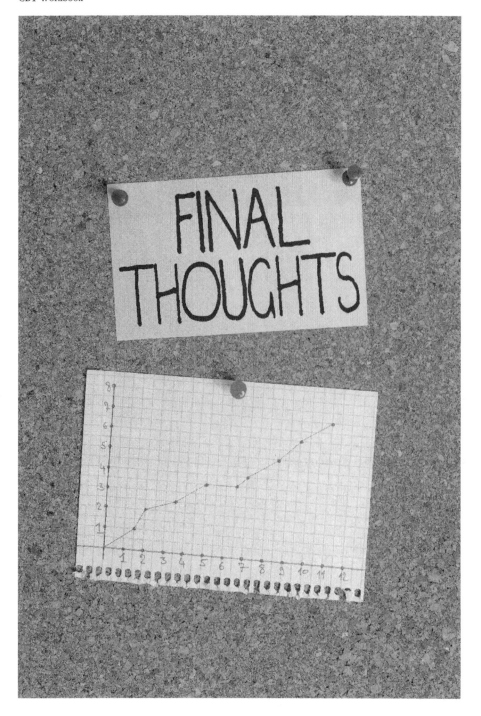

Conclusion

We have mainly concentrated on Cognitive Behavioral Therapy (CBT) as the foundation for addressing troubles in people's lives. Now, generate a list of the most significant problems or anxieties you'd like to focus on. Take note of how regularly they occur, if they are minor or serious, and how they influence your life. Use the workbook in the appendix at the end.

For example, someone might be feeling a sense of despair. To tackle this, they could keep track of how often these emotions occur, take note of how intrusive and disruptive they are, and note how this impacts their enjoyment of life and their overall outlook.

Depending on how quickly you have read through the content, you may still be experiencing fairly intense symptoms of your emotional struggles despite having read everything. It is important that you do not simply toss it aside and forget about it as you continue to face your daily struggles. Simply educating yourself on what needs to be done will not support you in healing. You will actually need to do the healing work. By remaining devoted and showing up for yourself every single day, you give yourself the attention that you need to truly embrace your healing journey with CBT.

It is important that you truly understand that self-healing does not mean isolating yourself from others. Isolating yourself is a common desire when you are experiencing something like anxiety or depression. However, doing so can impede your healing. Even on days where you do not feel like it, show up for yourself and attempt to make contact with at least one person per day who does not live with you. Doing so will support you in feeling a deeper sense of connection with those around you and will help you feel more attuned to the outside world.

You also need to make sure that you consistently practice your new mindfulness and CBT practices. Those who have recovered from psychological disorders using Cognitive Behavioral Therapy (CBT) are much less likely to relapse than those who are only being treated with medication. However, they may still be susceptible to experiencing a decline in their symptoms. By consistently monitoring your progress and staying informed with the necessary resources, you can better prepare yourself to tackle any challenges that may arise and prevent any potential relapses. Even if they do become problematic again, it is no reason to be ashamed.

Suppose you know of someone else who may benefit from CBT. The more that we can spread the message of healing and empower others to discover how they can heal themselves, the fewer people need to suffer from symptoms of anxiety and depression.

Hopefully, we have shown you that the negative outlook on life is merely a negative distortion of thought you can learn to surpass. To support you on your journey towards balanced positivity, we have included numerous exercises and introduced you to a number of techniques that support mental recovery. You learned how to use the thought record, one of the most important tools to examine your mind and track your progress. By learning how to use the thought record, you will be able to rationally evaluate every stressful situation and challenges that life throws at you. With that in mind, you can use this technique to beat automatic thoughts, rumination, dysfunctional beliefs, and assumptions, as well as to cope with fear and sadness.

Remember to stay open about your thoughts and experiences as much as possible. Communicating with your therapist openly, using detailed descriptions gives them the best insight into your experiences and helps them identify wrong beliefs and assumptions that are guiding your life. You've learned that the most likely cause for you to feel the way you do isn't in the fact that there is something wrong with you, because there isn't, but in the negative core beliefs that have shaped your perception of life. We have explained the definition and examples of core beliefs, helping you to understand how and why the unconscious mechanisms that are guiding you might be dysfunctional. Furthermore, we explained how and why the negative core beliefs cause cognitive distortions, automatic and intrusive thoughts that are bothering you the most. You now have guidance and instructions to stop nurturing these inadequate thinking patterns and shift towards positivity and clarity.

If your life has been affected by negative beliefs long enough, you may have learned how to use numerous avoidant, self-destructive behaviors. Without knowing it, you were relying on these behaviors to shelter yourself from fear. While avoiding stress might have worked for a while, you are going to have to work past these crippling, self-destructive behaviors in order to grow and change. We introduced graded exposure and behavioral activation as simple but effective techniques for you to gradually and patiently conquer your fears and introduce more enjoyable, positive behaviors into daily life.

*** BONUS 2 ***

As promised, I am happy to announce Bonus 2 "Time Management, Problem Solving and Critical Thinking."

These strategies will help you better manage your time and solve problems more efficiently. In addition, critical thinking is an essential skill that can help people make informed decisions.

What you learn will be very useful in both your personal and work life and can help you break out of the circle of overthinking. Studying these skills can help you develop greater awareness, save time, and be more productive. Follow us on this journey and discover how these skills can help you achieve success.

Have a great read!

https://BookHip.com/NWVFJJQ

Printed in Great Britain
by Amazon

24066758R00062